Understanding the Human Factor in Cyber Security: A Comprehensive Investigation

Christopher Stephenson

PUBLISHED BY:

Yahweh's Anointed Publishing
Jamaica, W.I.

AF719996

ISBN 978-976-97413-9-3

Published by: Yahweh's Anointed Publishing

Tel: 876-549-0063

Email: yahwehsanointedpublishing@gmail.com

Website: https://yapublishing.com

Contents

Abstract

In today's increasingly digital world, cybersecurity has become a cornerstone of modern society, safeguarding individuals, organizations, and governments against an ever-expanding range of cyber threats. Despite significant technological advancements, the **human factor** remains the weakest link in the cybersecurity chain. Whether due to negligence, lack of awareness, or malicious intent, human errors account for **74% of all breaches** (Verizon,2023). This research, *Understanding the Human Factor in Cybersecurity: A Comprehensive Investigation*, examines the pivotal role of human behavior in cybersecurity, providing an in-depth analysis of the psychological, behavioral, and organizational factors that contribute to vulnerabilities.

This research highlights the devastating consequences of human-related cybersecurity risks by analyzing real-world case studies, including the Target data breach, the Equifax breach, and the "WannaCry" ransomware attack. It examines common human errors, such as weak passwords, susceptibility to phishing attacks, insider threats, and system misconfigurations, while providing practical strategies to mitigate these risks. Key measures include **security awareness training**, **strong authentication mechanisms**, **fostering a security-first culture**, and **regular security audits**.

The research also explores the interplay between **technology and human behavior**, emphasizing the importance of user-friendly interfaces, automation, and human-machine collaboration. It addresses the role of **policy and regulation**, including the impact of the **General Data Protection Regulation (GDPR)** and the need for international cooperation and a standardized framework. Looking ahead, the book examines emerging trends such as **quantum computing**, the **Internet of Things (IoT)**, and the increasing demand for comprehensive **cybersecurity education**.

This research provides a comprehensive roadmap for addressing the human factor in cybersecurity by integrating psychological insights, technological advancements, and practical recommendations. It serves as an essential resource for cybersecurity professionals, organizational leaders, policymakers, and anyone seeking to understand and mitigate human-related risks. Ultimately, this book underscores that cybersecurity is not merely a technical challenge but a **human one**, requiring a proactive and holistic approach to build a resilient and secure digital environment.

Preface

The realm of cybersecurity is vast and complex, populated not only by codes and digital frameworks but also by the individuals who design, implement, and interact with these systems. This thesis, "Understanding the Human Factor in Cyber Security: A Comprehensive Investigation," seeks to bridge the gap between technical security solutions and the human elements that influence their effectiveness and vulnerabilities.

My interest in the intersection of human behavior and cybersecurity was sparked during my time working with a financial institution. There, I witnessed firsthand how, despite the presence of robust technical defenses, human errors often led to security breaches. This observation led me to the realization that understanding the human factor is not just a supplementary component of cybersecurity- it is central to developing effective security strategies.

Throughout this research, I have sought to explore various dimensions of human factors in cybersecurity, encompassing psychological, behavioral, and socio-technical aspects. The aim has been to provide a holistic view of how human behavior affects security protocols and how modifications in training and technology can help mitigate these risks. This investigation spans from the inadvertent mistakes made by users to the calculated psychological tactics employed by cyber attackers.

To conduct this investigation, my methodology centers around an extensive review of existing research conducted by leading professors in the field of cybersecurity. This was complemented by in-depth analyses of reports authored by industry experts following major corporate breaches. This approach has allowed me to synthesize diverse perspectives and data, offering a unique insight into the integration and impact of human factors on cybersecurity measures.

This thesis is dedicated to all cybersecurity professionals who strive daily to make the digital world safer for users. I hope this research fosters a deeper understanding of the human elements in cybersecurity and catalyzes further discussion and research in this critical area of study. I invite you to delve into the following chapters, where I examine these themes in detail, striving to enhance our collective knowledge and foster the creation of more secure cyber environments.

CHAPTER 1
Introduction

1.1 The Importance of Cybersecurity

In today's digital age, cybersecurity has become a cornerstone of modern society. As our reliance on digital technologies deepens, so does the complexity and frequency of cyber threats. The risks are vast and continuously evolving, from data breaches and ransomware attacks to sophisticated nation-state espionage. According to a report by Cybersecurity Ventures, the global cost of cybercrime is expected to reach $10.5 trillion annually by 2025, up from $3 trillion in 2015 (Morgan, 2020). This staggering increase underscores the urgent need for robust cybersecurity measures to protect individuals, organizations, and governments from the ever-growing threat of cyberattacks.

Cybersecurity is no longer just a technical challenge — it has become a critical concern for businesses and society alike. A single breach can inflict significant financial losses, irreparable reputational damage, regulatory penalties, and even jeopardize national security. For instance, the **2017 Equifax breach** compromised the personal information of 147 million people, resulting in a settlement of over **$700 million** and permanently tarnishing the company's reputation (Goodin, 2017). Similarly, the **2021 Colonial Pipeline ransomware attack** disrupted fuel supplies across the United States, starkly revealing the vulnerabilities of critical infrastructure to cyber threats (Turton, 2021).

The importance of cybersecurity extends beyond protecting data and systems—it is also about safeguarding trust. In an increasingly interconnected world, trust serves as the bedrock of digital interactions. Whether consumers entrust businesses with their personal information or governments rely on secure communication channels, cybersecurity is essential for maintaining this trust.

1.2 The Role of the Human Factor

While technological solutions -such as firewalls, encryption, and intrusion detection systems -are essential components of cybersecurity, they are not sufficient on their own. The **human factor, which includes** the behaviors, decisions, and interactions of individuals, plays a crucial role in determining the success and failure of cybersecurity efforts. Human errors- whether stemming from negligence, lack of awareness, or malicious intent- often represent the weakest link in the security chain.

Human behavior significantly influences cybersecurity outcomes, as illustrated in Figure 1.0, where psychological, social, and technical factors intersect.

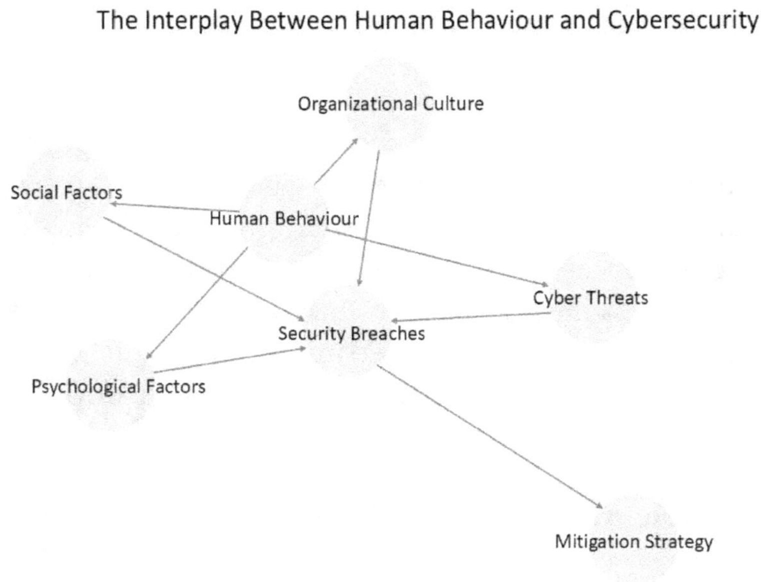

Figure 1.0 The interplay between human behaviour and cybersecurity vulnerabilities.

Phishing attacks, for example, which exploit social engineering tactics to deceive individuals into disclosing sensitive information, remain one of the most common and effective vectors. According to Verizon's **2023 Data Breach Investigations Report**, **74% of all breaches** involve the human element, including social engineering, errors, or misuse (Verizon, 2023). Similarly, **insider threats,** whether intentional or accidental, account for a significant share of cybersecurity incidents. Whether it is a disgruntled employee or a careless contractor, insider actions can be as devastating as those of an external hacker.

The human factor is inherently complex, as it requires understanding and influencing behavior shaped by psychological, social, and environmental factors. Cognitive biases, for instance, can significantly impact decision-making. **Optimism bias** - the belief that "it will not happen to me" and **confirmation bias** – the tendency to ignore evidence contradicting one's beliefs- often lead to poor security choices. Additionally, factors such as, stress, fatigue, and organizational culture shaping how play a pivotal role in h individuals perceive and respond to cybersecurity risks.

As Bruce Schneier, a renowned security expert, aptly put it, "**Security is not a product, but a process. It's a human process**" (Schneier, 2000). This insight highlights the critical need to address the human factor in cybersecurity. No matter how advanced the technology, it is ultimately people who design, deploy, and interact with these systems. Therefore, understanding and mitigating human-related risks is fundamental for building a resilient and secure digital environment.

1.3 Objectives and Scope of this research

This research aims to provide a **comprehensive investigation** into the human factor in cybersecurity. By examining real-world scenarios, psychological insights, and technological interactions, it seeks to understand the root causes behind human-related security vulnerabilities and propose actionable strategies to mitigate these risks effectively. The findings target a diverse, broad audience, including:

- **Cybersecurity professionals** seeking to enhance their understanding of human behavior and its influence on security.
- **Organizational leaders** are responsible for developing and implementing robust cybersecurity strategies.
- **Policymakers** are tasked with designing regulations and frameworks to address cybersecurity challenges.
- **Anyone interested** in understanding the human dimension of cybersecurity and its implications for individuals and society.

The scope of this research is wide-ranging, covering topics such as:

- The psychological and behavioral aspects of human behavior in cybersecurity.
- Real-world case studies that highlight the consequences of human errors.
- Common human-related mistakes, such as weak passwords habits, susceptibility to phishing attacks, and insider threats.
- Strategies for mitigating human-driven risks, including security awareness training, strong authentication mechanisms, and fostering a security first culture thinking.
- The role of policy and regulation in shaping cybersecurity practices.
- Future trends and challenges, such as the impact of quantum computing, the proliferation of IoT devices, and the growing need for widespread cybersecurity education.

By the end of this research, readers will have a deeper understanding of the human factor in cybersecurity and the tools and strategies needed to address it. The goal is to empower individuals and organizations to take a proactive approach to cybersecurity, recognizing that technology alone is not enough—people are the key to building a secure digital future.

CHAPTER 2
The Human Factor in Cybersecurity

The human factor in cybersecurity stands as one of the most crucial yet frequently underestimated components of safeguarding digital systems. While technological solutions—such as firewalls, encryption protocols, and intrusion detection systems—play a vital role, their effectiveness ultimately depends on the individuals who design, implement, and operate them. This chapter explores the human factor in depth, examining its definition, psychological foundations, and the pivotal ways in which human behavior can either fortify or compromise cybersecurity measures

2.1 Defining the Human Factor

The human factor in cybersecurity refers to the role that human behavior, decision-making, and interaction play in the security of information systems. This concept spans a broad spectrum of activities, from the behaviors of end-users, such as employees and customers, to the strategic decisions made by cybersecurity professionals. Unlike machines, humans are influenced by emotions, cognitive biases, social pressures, and environmental factors, making their behavior inherently unpredictable.

For example, a well-trained employee may still fall victim to a phishing attack when faced with stress or distractions. Similarly, a cybersecurity professional might inadvertently misconfigure a system due to overconfidence or a gap in awareness. These scenarios underscore the intricate nature of the human factor and its capacity to introduce vulnerabilities, even within the most secure systems.

2.2 Psychological Aspects of Human Behavior

Human behavior is deeply rooted in psychology, and understanding these psychological aspects is key to addressing the human factor in cybersecurity. Below are some of the most relevant psychological concepts:

Cognitive Biases

Cognitive biases and stress impair decision-making, creating vulnerabilities (see Figure 2.0).

They are systematic patterns of deviation from rationality in judgment. They often lead to errors in decision-making, which can have serious consequences for cybersecurity. Some common biases include:

- **Optimism Bias**: The tendency to believe that negative events (e.g., cyberattacks) are less likely to happen to oneself than to others. This can lead to complacency and a lack of preparedness (Tversky & Kahneman, 1974).
- **Confirmation Bias**: The tendency to seek out information that confirms pre-existing beliefs while ignoring contradictory evidence. For example, an IT administrator might dismiss a

security alert because it conflicts with their understanding of the system's safety.

- **Anchoring Effect**: The tendency to rely too heavily on the first piece of information encountered when making decisions. This can lead to poor risk assessments, such as underestimating the severity of a vulnerability.

Emotions and Stress

Emotions play a significant role in decision-making, with factors like stress, fatigue, and anxiety significantly impairing cognitive function and increasing vulnerability to mistakes. For instance, a stressed employee might overlook a phishing email's red flags or fail to follow proper security protocols. Research has shown that high-stress environments increase the likelihood of human error, which can be exploited by attackers (Reason, 1990).

Social Influences

Humans are inherently social beings, and their behavior is often influenced by the actions and opinions of others. For instance, employees might adopt lax security practices in a workplace setting if they perceive that their colleagues are not taking cybersecurity seriously. This phenomenon, known as social proof, can undermine organizational security efforts (Cialdini, 2001).

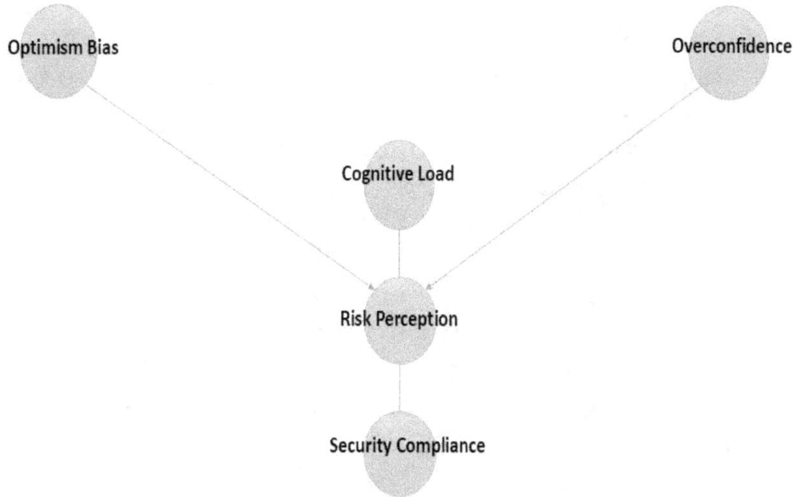

Figure 2.0 Psychological Factors Affecting Cybersecurity Behavior.

2.3 Social Engineering and Manipulation

Social engineering is a technique used by cybercriminals to manipulate individuals into divulging sensitive information or performing actions that compromise security. Unlike technical attacks, social engineering exploits human psychology, making it one of the most effective methods for breaching systems.

Common Social Engineering Tactics

- **Phishing**: Attackers send fraudulent emails or messages designed to trick recipients into revealing sensitive information, such as passwords or credit card numbers. Phishing attacks often impersonate trusted entities, such as banks or colleagues.

- **Pretexting**: Attackers fabricate a convincing scenario (pretext) to gain the victim's trust. For example, they might pose as an IT support technician and request login credentials to "fix" a non-existent issue.
- **Baiting**: Attackers offer something enticing, such as a free USB drive or software download, to lure victims into installing malware or providing sensitive information.
- **Tailgating**: Attackers physically follow an authorized person into a restricted area, such as secure office spaces, exploiting the human tendency to hold doors open for others.

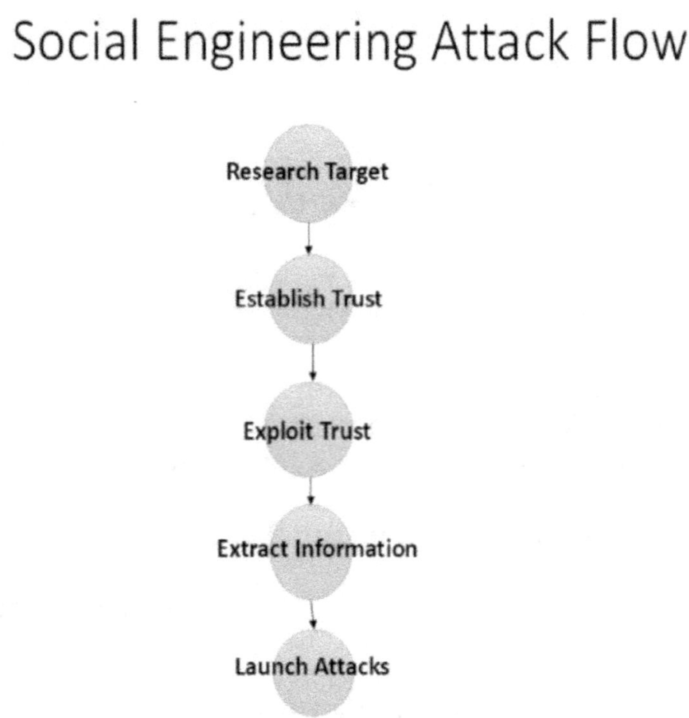

Figure 3.0 Social Engineering Attack lifecycle.

Figure 3.0 outlines the typical stages of a social engineering attack, from reconnaissance to exploitation.

Why Social Engineering Works

Social engineering leverages fundamental psychological traits, including trust, curiosity, and the innate desire to assist others. For example, people are more likely to comply with requests from authority figures, even if those requests seem unusual. This principle, known as the authority bias, is often exploited in phishing attacks where attackers impersonate executives or law enforcement officials (Hadnagy, 2010).

2.4 Cognitive Biases and Decision-Making

Cognitive biases significantly impact decision-making in cybersecurity, often leading to poor judgments and increased vulnerability. Below are some key biases and their implications:

Availability Heuristic

The availability heuristic is the tendency to make decisions based on readily available information rather than conducting a thorough analysis. For example, if an organization has not experienced a cyberattack in recent memory, employees may underestimate the likelihood of future attacks. This can lead to a false sense of security, leading to insufficient preparation and increased vulnerability.

Dunning-Kruger Effect

The Dunning-Kruger effect occurs when individuals with low ability in a particular area overestimate their competence. In cybersecurity, this can manifest as employees or even IT professionals believing they are more skilled at detecting threats than they are. This overconfidence can result in poor security practices and a failure to seek help when needed (Kruger & Dunning, 1999).

Overconfidence Bias

Overconfidence bias causes individuals to overestimate their knowledge or abilities, often resulting in risky decisions and behaviors. For instance, a developer might disable security features to speed up software deployment, mistakenly believing that their code is secure enough to withstand attacks. In the realm of cybersecurity, this bias poses significant dangers, as overconfidence can lead to catastrophic failures and expose systems to severe vulnerabilities.

Anchoring Effect

The anchoring effect occurs when individuals rely too heavily on the first piece of information they encounter when making decisions. In cybersecurity, this can lead to flawed risk assessments. For instance, if an organization's initial assessment of a vulnerability is overly optimistic, subsequent evaluations might be biased toward that initial judgment, even when presented with new and contradictory evidence.

2.5 The Role of Trust and Overconfidence

Trust and overconfidence are two interrelated factors that can significantly impact cybersecurity. While trust is essential for collaboration and efficiency, it also presents a vulnerability attackers can exploit. Overconfidence, in contrast, often breeds complacency, causing individuals or organizations to overlook critical risks.

Insider threats often follow a predictable cycle (Figure 4.0), beginning with access misuse and escalating to data exfiltration.

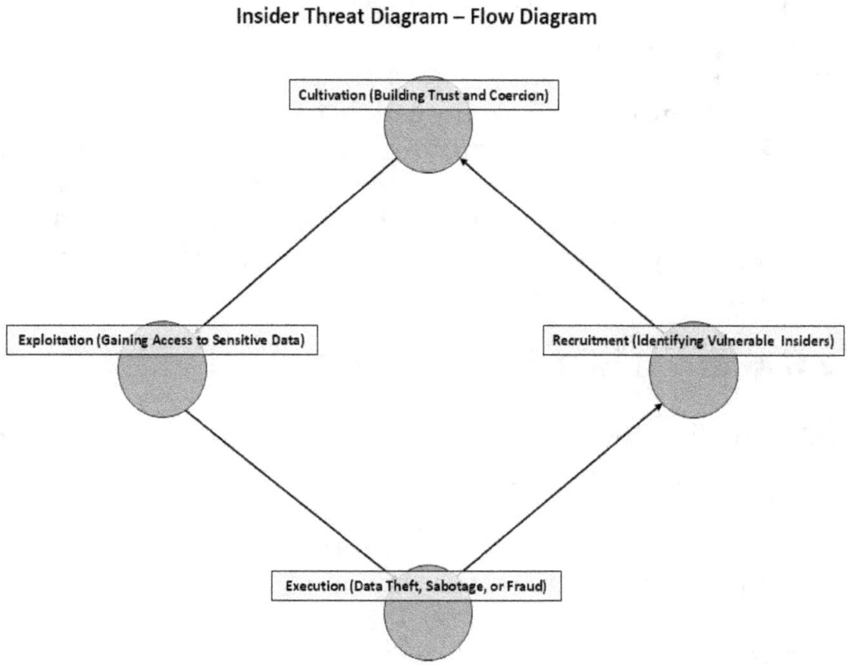

Figure 4.0 Insider Threat Lifecycle

Trust in Cybersecurity

Trust is a double-edged sword in cybersecurity. On one hand, trust is necessary for effective teamwork and communication. On the other hand, excessive trust can lead to vulnerabilities. For example, employees might instinctively trust emails from colleagues without verifying their authenticity, making them easy targets for phishing attacks. Similarly, organizations that rely on third-party vendors without rigorous security evaluations risk exposure to supply chain attacks.

Overconfidence in Cybersecurity

Overconfidence often fosters a false sense of security and insufficient preparedness. For example, an organization may assume that its existing security measures are robust enough to defend against all threats, leading to a reluctance to invest in additional safeguards. This overconfidence can also translate into a lack of emphasis on training and awareness, as both employees and IT professionals might mistakenly believe they possess adequate knowledge to remain secure.

2.6 Addressing the Human Factor

Effectively addressing the human factor in cybersecurity demands a well-rounded approach that integrates education, technology, and a strong organizational culture. Key strategies for mitigating human-related risks include:

Security Awareness Training

Regular training programs are vital in equipping employees to identify and respond to threats such as phishing and social engineering. To maximize their impact, training sessions should be engaging, practical, and tailored to the organization's specific needs.

Behavioral Nudges

Behavioral nudges, such as reminders to update passwords or warnings about suspicious emails, can help guide employees toward safer practices. These nudges leverage psychological principles to encourage positive behavior without being overly intrusive.

Fostering a Security-First Culture

Organizations should prioritize cybersecurity at all levels, from leadership to frontline employees. This includes promoting open communication about security concerns, rewarding good security practices, and holding individuals accountable for lapses.

Leveraging Technology

Technology offers powerful solutions to mitigate human errors, such as automating routine tasks, detecting anomalies, and delivering real-time feedback. For instance, AI-powered systems can monitor user behavior to uncover potential threats and proactively alert security teams, enabling quicker and more effective responses.

Conclusion

The human factor is a critical component of cybersecurity, influencing everything from individual behavior to organizational decision-making. By understanding the psychological and behavioral aspects of the human factor, organizations can develop more effective strategies for mitigating risks and enhancing security. While technology will continue to play a vital role in cybersecurity, addressing the human factor is essential for creating a resilient and secure digital environment.

CHAPTER 3: Real-World Scenarios and Case Studies

Understanding the human factor in cybersecurity is best achieved by examining real-world incidents where human behavior played a pivotal role. This chapter investigates five high-profile case studies, analyzing how human errors, psychological manipulation, and organizational culture contributed to significant cybersecurity breaches. These examples illustrate the importance of addressing the human factor to prevent similar incidents in the future.

3.1 The Target Data Breach (2013)

Overview

In 2013, retail giant Target suffered a massive data breach that exposed the credit card information of over 40 million customers and the personal data of 70 million individuals. The breach occurred during the busy holiday shopping season, causing significant financial and reputational damage to the company.

The Human Factor

The breach was initiated through a phishing email sent to a third-party HVAC vendor with access to Target's network. The attackers stole the vendor's credentials and used them to infiltrate Target's systems. Once inside, they installed malware on Target's point-of-sale (POS) systems to capture credit card data.

Key human-related issues included:

- **Third-Party Vulnerabilities**: Target failed to adequately monitor and secure its third-party vendors, highlighting the risks of over-reliance on external partners.
- **Lack of Security Awareness**: The HVAC vendor's employees fell victim to a phishing attack, demonstrating the importance of security awareness training for all parties with network access.
- **Delayed Response**: Target's security team ignored multiple warnings from its intrusion detection system, underscoring the dangers of complacency and overconfidence.

Lessons Learned

- Organizations must implement robust third-party risk management programs.
- Regular security awareness training is essential for all employees and contractors.
- Security teams must act promptly on alerts and warnings to mitigate potential threats.

3.2 The Equifax Breach (2017)

Overview

In 2017, Equifax, one of the largest credit reporting agencies, suffered a breach that exposed the personal information of 147 million people. The breach was attributed to the exploitation of a known vulnerability in the Apache Struts web application framework.

The Human Factor

The breach occurred because Equifax failed to patch the vulnerability despite a patch being available months earlier. The company's security team also failed to detect the breach for several weeks, allowing attackers to exfiltrate vast amounts of data.

Key human-related issues included:

- **Poor Patch Management**: Equifax's failure to apply the patch highlights the risks of neglecting basic cybersecurity hygiene.
- **Lack of Accountability**: The breach revealed a lack of clear responsibility for security within the organization, leading to critical oversights.
- **Inadequate Monitoring**: Equifax's security team failed to detect the breach in a timely manner, emphasizing the need for robust monitoring and incident response capabilities.

Lessons Learned

- Organizations must prioritize timely patch management and vulnerability remediation.
- Clear accountability and responsibility for cybersecurity are essential.
- Continuous monitoring and rapid incident response are critical for minimizing the impact of breaches.

3.3 The Sony Pictures Hack (2014)

Overview

In 2014, Sony Pictures Entertainment was targeted by a sophisticated cyberattack attributed to North Korean hackers. The attackers stole and leaked sensitive data, including unreleased films, confidential employee information, and internal communications.

The Human Factor

The attackers gained access to Sony's network through spear-phishing emails sent to employees. Once inside, they deployed malware to exfiltrate data and cripple Sony's systems.

Key human-related issues included:

- **Spear-Phishing**: Employees fell victim to highly targeted phishing emails, demonstrating the effectiveness of social engineering tactics.
- **Weak Password Practices**: The attackers escalated their access by exploiting weak passwords and poor password management practices.
- **Lack of Preparedness**: Sony's incident response was slow and disorganized, exacerbating the damage caused by the breach.

Lessons Learned

- Organizations must implement advanced email security measures to detect and block phishing attempts.
- Strong password policies and multi-factor authentication are essential for preventing unauthorized access.
- A well-defined incident response plan is critical for minimizing the impact of breaches.

3.4 The "WannaCry" Ransomware Attack (2017)

Overview

In 2017, the "WannaCry" ransomware attack affected hundreds of thousands of computers worldwide, including those of the UK's National Health Service (NHS). The attack encrypted files and demanded ransom payments in Bitcoin, causing widespread disruption.

The Human Factor

"WannaCry" exploited a vulnerability in Microsoft Windows that had been patched months earlier. However, many organizations, including the NHS, had failed to apply the patch, leaving their systems vulnerable.

Key human-related issues included:

- **Poor Patch Management**: Failing to apply the patch highlights the risks of neglecting basic cybersecurity practices.
- **Lack of Awareness**: Many organizations were unaware of the vulnerability or underestimated its severity, leading to inadequate preparation.
- **Overreliance on Legacy Systems**: The NHS's reliance on outdated systems made it particularly vulnerable to the attack.

Lessons Learned

- Organizations must prioritize timely patch management and vulnerability remediation.
- Regular security audits and risk assessments are essential for identifying and addressing vulnerabilities.
- Upgrading outdated systems and infrastructure is critical for maintaining a strong security posture.

3.5 The Twitter Bitcoin Scam (2020)

Overview

In July 2020, a high-profile Twitter hack compromised several verified accounts, including those of Barack Obama, Elon Musk, and Bill Gates. The attackers used the compromised accounts to post fraudulent tweets promoting a Bitcoin scam.

The Human Factor

The attackers gained access to Twitter's internal systems through social engineering tactics, targeting employees with access to administrative tools. Once inside, they used these tools to take control of high-profile accounts.

Key human-related issues included:

- **Insider Threats**: The attackers exploited the trust placed in employees with access to sensitive systems, highlighting the risks of insider threats.
- **Social Engineering**: The attackers used social engineering to manipulate employees into providing access credentials, demonstrating the effectiveness of psychological manipulation.
- **Lack of Access Controls**: Twitter's internal systems lacked sufficient access controls, allowing the attackers to escalate their privileges and take control of accounts.

Lessons Learned

- Organizations must implement robust access controls and monitor privileged accounts.
- Regular security awareness training is essential for preventing social engineering attacks.
- Insider threat detection and mitigation programs are critical for protecting sensitive systems.

Conclusion

These real-world scenarios underscore the critical role of the human factor in cybersecurity. From phishing attacks and poor patch management to insider threats and social engineering, human behavior frequently emerges as the most vulnerable point in the security framework. By analyzing these incidents, organizations can extract valuable lessons and devise more effective strategies to lessen human-related risks, ultimately strengthening their overall security posture.

The cascading effects of breaches, as depicted in Figure 5, highlight financial, reputational, and operational impacts

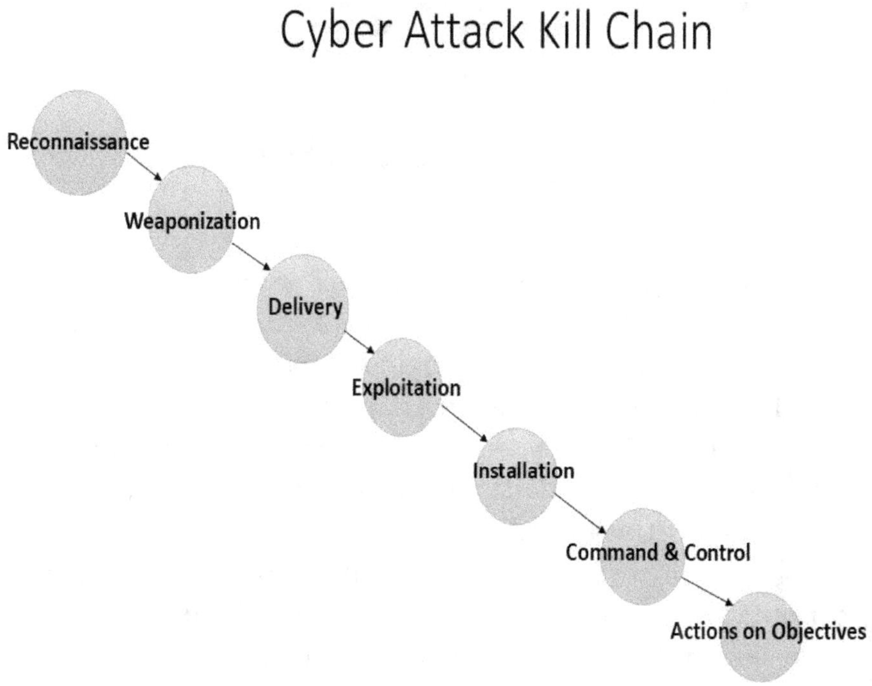

Figure 5. Consequences of major data breaches

CHAPTER 4: Common Human Errors in Cybersecurity

As previously emphasized, human errors remain one of the most substantial factors behind cybersecurity breaches. Despite technological advancements, people continue to be the most fragile element in the defense system. This chapter explores the most common human errors in cybersecurity, their underlying causes, and their potential consequences. By gaining deeper insights into these errors, organizations can formulate targeted approaches to mitigate risks and strengthen their overall protective infrastructure.

4.1 Password Management Issues

Overview

Weak or reused passwords are a pervasive problem in cybersecurity. Many users opt for easily guessable passwords or reuse the same password across multiple accounts, making it easier for attackers to gain unauthorized access.

Common Password-Related Errors

- **Weak Passwords**: Users often create passwords that are easy to remember but also easy to guess, such as "123456" or "password."
- **Password Reuse**: Using the same password across multiple accounts increases the risk of a

breach. If one account is compromised, attackers can use the same credentials to access other accounts.

- **Failure to Update Passwords**: Many users fail to update their passwords regularly, leaving accounts vulnerable to brute-force attacks.

Real-World Example

In 2012, LinkedIn suffered a data breach that exposed 6.5 million user passwords. The breach was attributed to weak password hashing, but many of the compromised passwords were found to be weak or reused across multiple accounts.

Mitigation Strategies

- Implement strong password policies that require complex, unique passwords.
- Encourage the use of password managers to generate and store secure passwords.
- Educate users about the risks of password reuse and the importance of regular password updates.

4.2 Phishing Attacks

Overview

Phishing attacks continue to be one of the most successful tactics for compromising security. These attacks rely on social engineering techniques to trick users into revealing sensitive information or clicking on malicious links. ***Phishing attacks evolve through***

distinct phases (Figure 7), from baiting to credential harvesting.

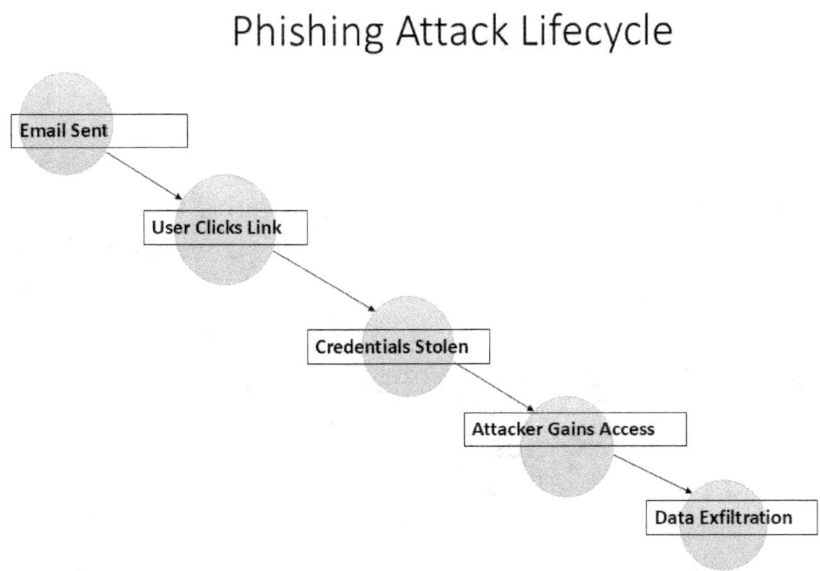

Figure 7. Phishing attack lifecycle.

Common Phishing-Related Errors

- **Falling for Phishing Emails**: Users often fail to recognize phishing emails, especially when they are well-crafted and appear to come from trusted sources.
- **Clicking on Malicious Links**: Users may inadvertently click on malicious links in phishing emails, which can lead to malware infections or credential theft.
- **Providing Sensitive Information**: Phishing attacks often prompt users to provide sensitive

information, such as login credentials or financial details.

Real-World Example

In 2016, the Democratic National Committee (DNC) suffered a phishing attack that led to the theft and leak of sensitive emails. The attackers used spear-phishing emails to trick DNC staff into revealing their credentials.

Mitigation Strategies

- Conduct regular security awareness training to help users recognize and respond to phishing attempts.
- Implement advanced email security measures like spam filters and phishing detection tools.
- Use multi-factor authentication (MFA) to reduce the risk of credential theft.

4.3 Insider Threats

Overview

Whether intentional or accidental, insider threats pose a significant risk to organizations. Malicious insiders may intentionally steal or leak sensitive information for personal gain or sabotage, while negligent insiders may inadvertently expose data through careless behavior.

Common Insider Threat-Related Errors

- **Unauthorized Access**: Employees may access sensitive information without proper authorization out of curiosity or malicious intent.

- **Data Leakage**: Insiders may inadvertently leak sensitive data through email, file-sharing services, or social media.
- **Sabotage**: Disgruntled employees may intentionally sabotage systems or compromise data, causing substantial harm to the organization's operations and reputation.

Real-World Example

In 2017, a former employee of Tesla was found to have stolen sensitive data and shared it with third parties. The employee had access to the data as part of their job, but misused it for personal gain.

Mitigation Strategies

- Implement strict access controls to limit access to sensitive information.
- Monitor user activity for signs of unauthorized access or data leakage.
- Conduct regular security audits and background checks on employees with access to sensitive data.

4.4 Lack of Security Awareness

Overview

Employees' lack of security awareness is a major contributor to cybersecurity vulnerabilities. Many users are unaware of the risks associated with their actions, such as clicking on suspicious links or downloading unverified attachments. This gap in awareness underscores the need for comprehensive training programs and clear organizational policies to foster a culture of security mindfulness.

Common Security Awareness-Related Errors

- **Ignoring Security Policies**: Employees may ignore or bypass security policies, such as using personal devices for work or connecting to unsecured networks.
- **Failure to Report Incidents**: Employees may fail to report security incidents, such as phishing attempts or malware infections, due to a lack of awareness or fear of repercussions.
- **Poor Cyber Hygiene**: Employees may use poor cyber hygiene practices, such as using weak passwords or failing to update software.

Real-World Example

In 2019, the city of Baltimore suffered a ransomware attack that disrupted city services for weeks. The attack was attributed to a lack of security awareness among city employees, who failed to recognize and respond to phishing attempts.

Mitigation Strategies

- Conduct regular security awareness training to educate employees about cybersecurity risks and best practices.
- Promote a culture of security where employees feel comfortable reporting incidents and seeking help.
- Implement policies and procedures that reinforce good cyber hygiene practices.

4.5 Misconfiguration and Poor Patch Management

Overview

Misconfigured systems and unpatched software are common entry points for attackers. Many organizations fail to properly configure their security settings or apply patches in a timely manner, leaving their systems vulnerable to exploitation.

Common Misconfiguration and Patch Management-Related Errors

- **Default Settings**: Many systems are deployed with default settings, which may include weak security configurations.
- **Unpatched Vulnerabilities**: Organizations may fail to apply patches for known vulnerabilities, leaving systems exposed to exploitation.
- **Lack of Monitoring**: Organizations may fail to monitor their systems for signs of

misconfiguration or vulnerabilities, leading to undetected security gaps.

Real-World Example

In 2017, the Equifax breach was attributed to a failure to patch a known vulnerability in the Apache Struts web application framework. The unpatched vulnerability allowed attackers to infiltrate Equifax's systems and steal sensitive data.

Mitigation Strategies

- Implement a robust patch management process to ensure timely application of security updates.
- Conduct regular security audits to identify and address misconfigurations.
- Use automated tools to monitor systems for vulnerabilities and misconfigurations.

Conclusion

Human errors are a critical yet frequently underestimated aspect of cybersecurity. Issues such as weak passwords, phishing attacks, insider threats, and poor patch management can have severe consequences for organizations, from data breaches to financial and reputational damage. By identifying and understanding these common human vulnerabilities, organizations can implement targeted mitigation strategies to address them effectively. This proactive approach is essential for minimizing risks and strengthening overall security resilience.

CHAPTER 5
Psychological and Behavioral Insights

Understanding the psychological and behavioral dimensions of human behavior is essential for tackling the human factor in cybersecurity. Decision-making processes are often shaped by cognitive biases, emotional responses, and social dynamics, which can contribute to errors and vulnerabilities. This chapter explores these psychological and behavioral insights, providing a deeper understanding of how they impact cybersecurity and offering strategies to counter their effects.

5.1 The Role of Stress and Fatigue

Overview

Stress and fatigue are significant factors that can impair cognitive function and decision-making. In high-pressure environments, individuals are more likely to make mistakes, overlook critical details, and fall victim to social engineering attacks.

Stress degrades situational awareness, increasing susceptibility to errors (Figure 8).

Impact on Cybersecurity

- **Reduced Vigilance**: Stressed or fatigued employees are less likely to notice suspicious activity, such as phishing emails or unauthorized access attempts.

- **Impaired Judgment**: Stress can lead to poor decision-making, such as bypassing security protocols to meet tight deadlines.
- **Increased Susceptibility to Social Engineering**: Fatigue can make individuals more susceptible to manipulation, as they are less likely to critically evaluate requests or communications.

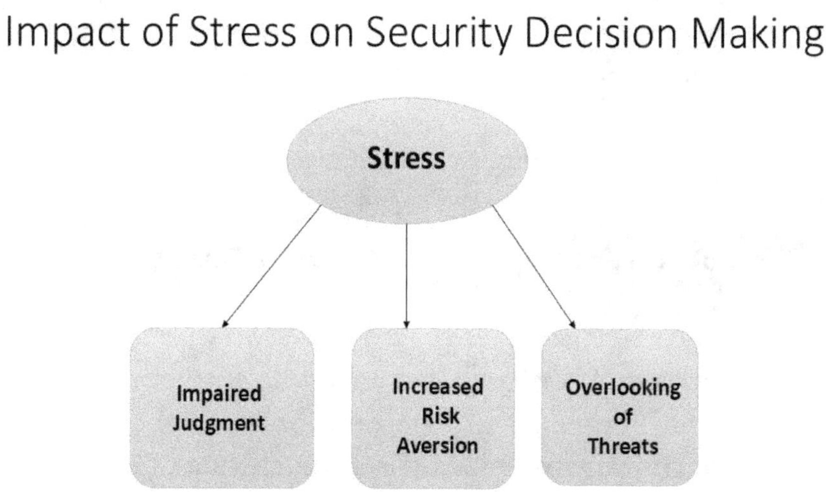

Figure 8. Impact of stress on security decision-making

Real-World Example

In 2015, the U.S. Office of Personnel Management (OPM) suffered a data breach that exposed the personal information of 21.5 million individuals. The breach was attributed to a combination of technical vulnerabilities and human errors, including the failure of overworked IT staff to detect and respond to the attack.

Mitigation Strategies

- Promote a healthy work-life balance to reduce stress and fatigue.
- Implement policies that encourage regular breaks and time off.
- Provide resources and support for stress management, including counseling and wellness programs.

5.2 The Impact of Organizational Culture

Overview

Organizational culture is a critical factor in influencing employee behavior and perceptions of cybersecurity. A culture that emphasizes the importance of security and promotes open dialogue about potential threats fosters a proactive stance toward identifying and mitigating risks. By embedding cybersecurity awareness into the core of organizational values, companies can empower employees to prioritize safety and collectively strengthen defenses against evolving threats.

Impact on Cybersecurity

- **Security-First Culture**: Organizations that prioritize security at all levels are more likely to have employees who follow best practices and report potential threats.
- **Blame Culture**: A culture that punishes employees for reporting security incidents can lead to underreporting and increased vulnerability.
- **Complacency**: A lack of emphasis on security can result in complacency, where employees underestimate risks and fail to take necessary precautions.

Real-World Example

In 2017, the Equifax breach was exacerbated by a lack of accountability and a culture that did not prioritize security. The breach revealed significant gaps in the company's security practices, including failing to patch a known vulnerability.

Mitigation Strategies

- Foster a culture of security where employees feel empowered to report incidents and seek help.
- Encourage open communication and collaboration on security issues.
- Recognize and reward employees who demonstrate good security practices.

5.3 The Dunning-Kruger Effect in Cybersecurity

Overview

The Dunning-Kruger effect is a cognitive bias where individuals with low ability in a particular area overestimate their competence. In cybersecurity, this can lead to overconfidence and poor decision-making.

Impact on Cybersecurity

- **Overconfidence**: Employees who overestimate their ability to detect and respond to threats may engage in risky behavior, such as ignoring security alerts or bypassing protocols.
- **Lack of Training**: Individuals affected by the Dunning-Kruger effect may be less likely to seek training or assistance, believing they already possess the necessary skills.
- **Increased Vulnerability**: Overconfidence can lead to a false sense of security, making organizations more vulnerable to attacks.

Real-World Example

In 2014, the Sony Pictures hack was facilitated by employees who fell victim to spear-phishing emails. The attackers exploited the overconfidence of employees who believed they could recognize and avoid phishing attempts.

Mitigation Strategies

- Provide regular training and education to help employees accurately assess their skills and knowledge.

- Encourage a culture of continuous learning and improvement.
- Use simulations and exercises to test employees' ability to recognize and respond to threats.

5.4 The Role of Trust and Overconfidence

Overview

Trust and overconfidence are closely connected and have a profound influence on cybersecurity. Although trust is crucial for fostering teamwork and operational efficiency, it also creates opportunities for exploitation by malicious actors. Similarly, overconfidence often results in complacency, leaving risks unnoticed or underestimated.

Impact on Cybersecurity

- **Exploitation of Trust**: Attackers often exploit trust to gain access to systems and information. For example, phishing emails that appear to come from trusted sources are more likely to be successful.
- **Complacency**: Overconfidence in one's ability to detect and respond to threats can lead to complacency, where individuals fail to take necessary precautions.
- **Insider Threats**: Excessive trust in employees or third-party vendors can increase the risk of insider threats, where individuals misuse their access for malicious purposes.

Real-World Example

In 2020, the Twitter Bitcoin scam involved attackers exploiting the trust placed in employees with access to administrative tools. The attackers used social engineering to manipulate employees into providing access credentials, which they then used to take control of high-profile accounts.

Mitigation Strategies

- Implement robust access controls and monitor privileged accounts.
- Conduct regular security awareness training to educate employees about the risks of social engineering.
- Foster a culture of healthy skepticism, where employees are encouraged to verify requests and communications.

5.5 Cognitive Biases and Decision-Making

Overview

Cognitive biases are consistent patterns of irrational judgment that can skew decision-making. These biases often result in errors, which may have significant implications for cybersecurity by increasing vulnerabilities and influencing critical decisions.

Common Cognitive Biases in Cybersecurity

As mentioned in Chapter 2:

- **Optimism Bias**: Leads individuals to believe they are less likely to experience negative events compared to others. In cybersecurity, it may result in underestimating the likelihood of falling victim to cyberattacks.
- **Confirmation Bias**: Drives individuals to favor information that aligns with their existing beliefs while disregarding evidence that contradicts them. In cybersecurity, it can lead to overlooking potential threats.
- **Anchoring Effect**: Occurs when individuals rely too heavily on the first piece of information they receive (the "anchor") when making decisions. In cybersecurity, this bias might lead professionals to underestimate new threats if their initial assessment of a system's security was overly optimistic.

Real-World Example

In 2017, the WannaCry ransomware attack exploited a known vulnerability in Microsoft Windows that had been patched months earlier. Many organizations failed to apply the patch due to the anchoring effect, where they relied on initial assessments that underestimated the risk.

Mitigation Strategies

- Provide training on cognitive biases and their impact on decision-making.
- Encourage a culture of critical thinking and evidence-based decision-making.

- Use data and analytics to support risk assessments and decision-making.

Conclusion

Psychological and behavioral insights offer valuable perspectives on the human factor in cybersecurity. By understanding how stress, organizational culture, cognitive biases, and overconfidence influence behavior, organizations can devise focused strategies to reduce human-related risks. Tackling these psychological and behavioral elements is crucial for fostering a robust and secure digital ecosystem. ---

CHAPTER 6: Technological and Human Interaction

The interaction between humans and technology plays a pivotal role in cybersecurity. Although technological solutions are indispensable for safeguarding digital systems, their success largely depends on how humans design, implement, and utilize them. This chapter examines the intricate relationship between technology and human behavior, focusing on how user interface design, automation, and human-machine collaboration can bolster or weaken cybersecurity efforts.

6.1 User Interface Design and Usability

Overview

User interface (UI) design is a vital component of cybersecurity. An intuitive, thoughtfully designed interface simplifies the process for users to adhere to security protocols, reducing the likelihood of mistakes. Conversely, a poorly designed UI can create confusion and lead to errors, exposing systems to vulnerabilities and potential breaches.

Impact on Cybersecurity

- **Complexity and Confusion**: Complex or unintuitive interfaces can confuse users, increasing the likelihood of errors such as misconfiguring security settings or disregarding critical warnings. Simplified, user-friendly designs are essential to minimize these risks and support secure decision-making.

- **Security Fatigue**: Overly burdensome security measures, such as frequent password changes or multi-step authentication processes, can lead to security fatigue, where users become desensitized to security prompts and bypass them.
- **Error-Prone Design**: Poorly designed interfaces can increase the likelihood of user errors, such as clicking on malicious links or downloading unverified attachments.

Real-World Example

In 2017, a misconfigured Amazon S3 bucket led to the exposure of sensitive data for millions of Verizon customers. The misconfiguration was attributed to the complexity of the S3 interface, which made it difficult for users to configure security settings properly.

Mitigation Strategies

- Apply user-centered design principles to create intuitive and user-friendly interfaces.
- Simplify security processes to reduce the burden on users and minimize the risk of errors.
- Provide clear and concise instructions for configuring security settings.

6.2 The Role of Automation and AI

Overview

Automation and artificial intelligence (AI) are becoming key drivers in advancing cybersecurity efforts. These technologies are central to minimizing human-related risks by alleviating user burdens and streamlining security processes. By enhancing accuracy and efficiency, automation and AI contribute to stronger defenses against evolving threats.

MFA adds critical verification layers (Figure 9), mitigating credential theft risks.

Impact on Cybersecurity

- **Threat Detection**: AI-powered systems can analyze vast amounts of data to detect anomalies and identify potential threats in real-time.
- **Incident Response**: Automation can streamline incident response processes, enabling organizations to quickly contain and mitigate security incidents.
- **Bias and Errors**: AI can enhance cybersecurity but is not immune to errors. Biased or flawed algorithms can lead to false positives or negatives, undermining security efforts.

Real-World Example

In 2019, Capital One suffered a data breach that exposed the personal information of over 100 million customers. The breach was attributed to a misconfigured web application firewall, which was supposed to be managed by an automated system. The incident highlighted the risks of over-reliance on automation without proper oversight.

Mitigation Strategies

- Use AI and automation to augment, rather than replace, human expertise. By combining human intuition and judgment with the efficiency and precision of automated systems, organizations can create a balanced and effective cybersecurity strategy.
- Conduct frequent audits and tests of AI systems to verify their accuracy, ensure proper functioning, and identify potential biases. This proactive approach helps maintain their reliability and fairness.
- Provide security professionals with training on how to use and manage automated systems effectively. This equips professionals with the necessary skills to maximize system capabilities, troubleshoot issues, and optimize performance while minimizing risks.

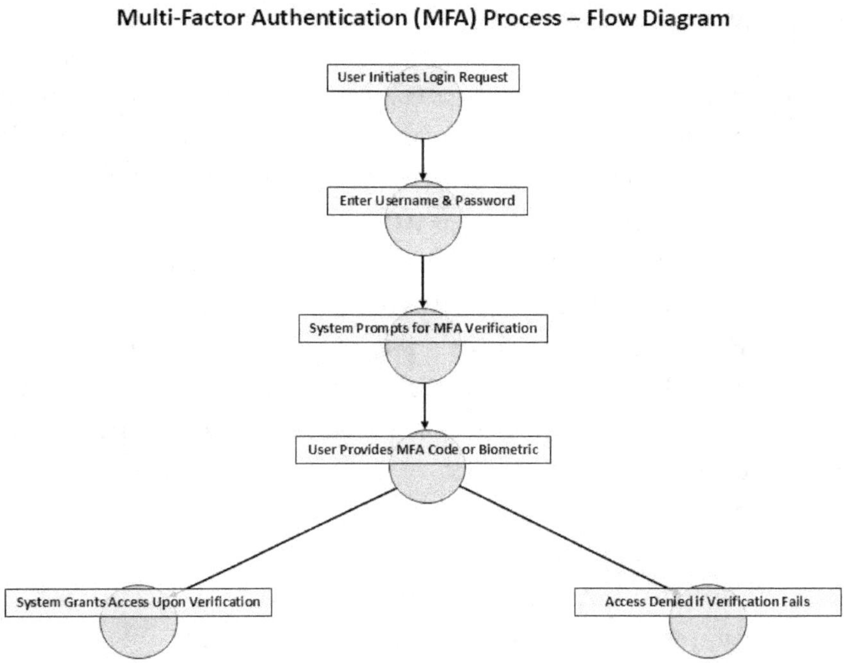

Figure 9. Multi-factor authentication workflow.

6.3 Human-Machine Collaboration

Overview

Effective cybersecurity hinges on the synergy between human expertise and machine capabilities. While machines excel at processing massive datasets and detecting patterns that signal potential threats, human insight is indispensable for interpreting these findings and making well-informed decisions. By combining the strengths of both, organizations can establish a more robust and adaptive security framework.

Impact on Cybersecurity

- **Enhanced Decision-Making**: Human-machine collaboration can enhance decision-making by combining the analytical capabilities of machines with the contextual understanding of humans. This synergy enables more accurate threat assessments and informed responses.
- **Reduced Workload**: Automation can reduce the workload of security professionals, allowing them to focus on more complex tasks and enhancing overall efficiency and effectiveness in cybersecurity operations.
- **Improved Accuracy**: Human oversight can help identify and correct errors made by automated systems, improving overall accuracy.

Real-World Example

In 2020, the SolarWinds supply chain attack was detected through a combination of automated threat detection and human analysis. Automated systems flagged unusual activity, which security professionals then investigated to uncover the full extent of the breach.

Mitigation Strategies

- Foster collaboration between humans and machines by integrating automated systems with human oversight. This approach ensures that machines complement human expertise, while human judgment mitigates potential errors, creating a balanced and efficient cybersecurity framework.

- Provide training for security professionals on how to effectively collaborate with automated systems. This equips them with the skills to leverage automation, understand its capabilities and limitations, and foster seamless integration between human expertise and machine efficiency.
- Use human-machine collaboration to enhance threat detection, incident response, and decision-making. By combining the speed and precision of automated systems with the contextual understanding and critical judgment of humans, organizations can create a more effective and adaptive cybersecurity strategy.

6.4 The Future of Human-Centric Cybersecurity

Overview

As technology continues to evolve, the role of the human factor in cybersecurity will become increasingly important. Emerging trends, such as the widespread adoption of IoT devices and the advent of quantum computing, will introduce new challenges and opportunities. These developments underscore the need for a human-centric approach to cybersecurity, ensuring that systems are technologically robust and thoughtfully designed to account for human behavior and decision-making.

Impact on Cybersecurity

- **IoT Security**: The proliferation of IoT devices will increase the complexity of cybersecurity, requiring new approaches to secure these devices and the data they generate.
- **Quantum Computing**: Quantum computing has the potential to break current encryption algorithms, necessitating the development of quantum-resistant encryption methods.
- **AI and Machine Learning**: Advances in AI and machine learning will continue to enhance cybersecurity, but will also introduce new risks, such as adversarial attacks and biased algorithms.

Real-World Example

In 2021, the Colonial Pipeline ransomware attack highlighted the vulnerabilities of critical infrastructure to cyber threats. The attack disrupted fuel supplies across the U.S. and underscored the need for robust cybersecurity measures to protect critical infrastructure.

Mitigation Strategies

- Stay informed about emerging technologies and their impact on cybersecurity.
- Invest in research and development to address new challenges, such as IoT security and quantum-resistant encryption.

- Foster a culture of continuous learning and adaptation to keep pace with technological advancements.

Conclusion

The interaction between humans and technology is a critical aspect of cybersecurity. By understanding the impact of user interface design, automation, and human-machine collaboration, organizations can develop more effective strategies to temper risks stemming from human behavior. Addressing the human factor will be essential for creating a resilient and secure digital ecosystem as technology progresses.

CHAPTER 7: Strategies for Mitigating Human-Related Risks

Human-related risks represent some of the most significant challenges in cybersecurity. Although technological solutions are indispensable, they must be complemented by strategies that address the human element. This chapter examines various approaches to mitigate human-related risks, including implementing security awareness training, establishing robust authentication mechanisms, cultivating a security-first culture, conducting regular security audits, and developing comprehensive incident response plans. Together, these strategies aim to minimize human errors and strengthen organizations' overall security framework.

7.1 Security Awareness Training

Overview

Security awareness training is one of the most effective ways to mitigate human-related risks. This training enables employees to identify, understand, and effectively respond to cybersecurity risks by equipping them with knowledge about potential threats and best practices. It fosters a proactive approach to safeguarding organizational assets and reinforces a culture of vigilance against emerging threats.

Key Components

- **Phishing Awareness**: Training employees to recognize and avoid phishing emails is crucial, as phishing remains one of the most common attack vectors. Through targeted training, employees can learn to recognize red flags, such as suspicious email addresses, unexpected attachments, and urgent requests for sensitive information, significantly reducing the risk of falling victim to such attacks.
- **Password Management**: Teaching employees the importance of creating strong, unique passwords and the risks associated with reusing passwords across multiple platforms is crucial. Effective training emphasizes techniques such as using passphrases, incorporating a mix of characters, and leveraging password managers to securely generate and store complex passwords, reducing the risk of unauthorized access.
- **Social Engineering**: Educating employees about the tactics used in social engineering attacks and equipping them with strategies to verify the authenticity of requests is vital. Training should focus on recognizing manipulation techniques, such as urgency, flattery, or impersonation, and verifying requests through trusted channels before sharing sensitive information or granting access. These skills help employees become the

first line of defense against social engineering schemes.

- **Incident Reporting**: Encouraging employees to report security incidents promptly, without fear of reprisal. Effective training emphasizes creating a supportive environment where employees feel empowered to share concerns promptly. By fostering a no-blame culture and ensuring clear, accessible reporting channels, organizations can respond swiftly to potential threats and mitigate risks more effectively.

Implementation Tips

- Conduct regular training sessions to ensure employees stay aware of evolving cybersecurity threats and best practices.
- Use simulations, such as mock phishing exercises, to reinforce learning.
- Tailor training programs to the specific needs and risks of the organization. Personalized content increases relevance and effectiveness, ensuring the program addresses real-world challenges.

Effective training follows a cyclical model (Figure 10), integrating assessment, delivery, and reinforcement.

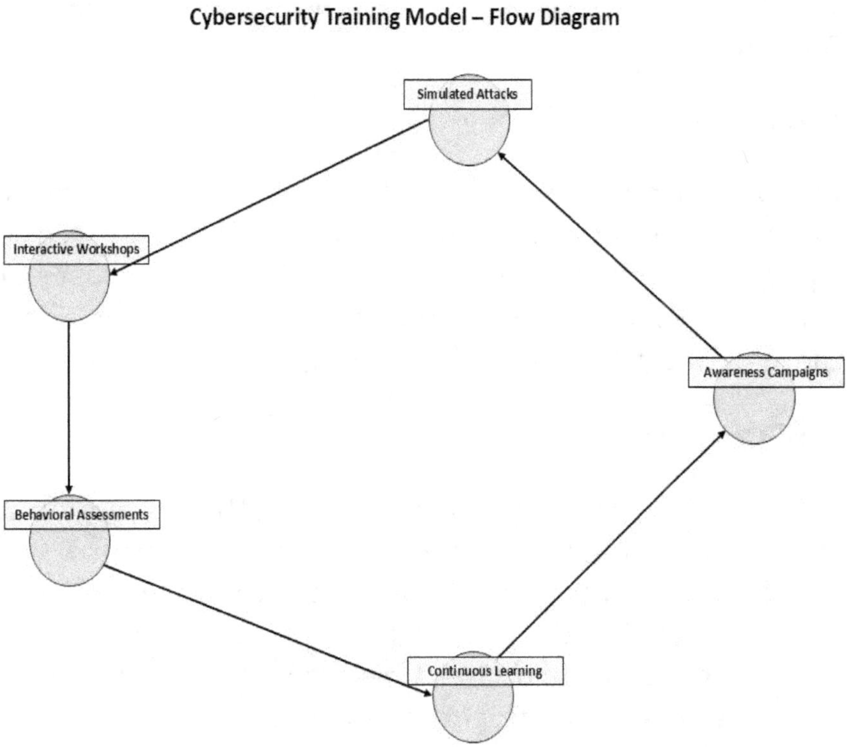

Figure 10. Cybersecurity training framework.

Real-World Example

After implementing a comprehensive security awareness training program, a financial services company saw a 50% reduction in phishing incidents within six months. The training included interactive modules, regular quizzes, and simulated phishing attacks.

7.2 Implementing Strong Authentication Mechanisms

Overview

Strong authentication mechanisms, such as multi-factor authentication (MFA), can significantly reduce the risk of unauthorized access. MFA requires users to provide two or more forms of verification, making it more difficult for attackers to compromise accounts.

Key Components

- **Multi-Factor Authentication (MFA)**: Combining something the user knows (e.g., a password) with something the user has (e.g., a mobile device) or something the user is (e.g., a fingerprint).
- **Biometric Authentication**: Using biometric data, such as fingerprints or facial recognition, to enhance security.
- **Single Sign-On (SSO)**: Allowing users to access multiple systems with a single set of credentials, reducing the risk of password fatigue and reuse.

Implementation Tips

- Implement MFA for all critical systems and accounts.
- Educate users about the importance of MFA and how to use it effectively.
- Regularly review and update authentication mechanisms to address emerging threats.

Real-World Example

Google reported that enabling MFA blocked 100% of automated bot attacks and 99% of bulk phishing attacks. This highlights the effectiveness of strong authentication mechanisms in mitigating human-related risks.

7.3 Developing a Security-First Culture

Overview

A security-first culture prioritizes cybersecurity at all levels of the organization, from leadership to frontline employees. It fosters an environment where every individual understands the importance of security and takes ownership of their role in protecting organizational assets. Integrating security into daily operations and decision-making processes ensures that cybersecurity is viewed not as a standalone effort but as a shared responsibility.

Key Components

- **Leadership Commitment**: Leaders must demonstrate a commitment to cybersecurity by allocating resources, setting policies, and leading by example.
- **Employee Engagement**: Encouraging employees to take an active role in cybersecurity by reporting incidents and following best practices.

- **Open Communication**: Creating a culture where employees feel comfortable discussing security concerns and reporting incidents without fear of punishment.

Implementation Tips

- Develop and communicate clear security policies and procedures.
- Recognize and reward employees who demonstrate good security practices.
- Conduct regular security briefings and updates to keep security at the forefront of people's minds.

Real-World Example

A technology company implemented a security-first culture by integrating cybersecurity into its core values. The company conducted regular security training, established a security champions program, and encouraged open communication about security issues. As a result, the company saw a significant reduction in security incidents and improved employee engagement.

7.4 Zero Trust model

The Zero Trust model is a security framework that operates on the principle: "Never trust, always verify." It assumes that threats can exist both inside and outside an organization's network, so no user or device is automatically trusted, even if they are within the traditional network perimeter.

Key Principles of Zero Trust:

1. **Verify Explicitly**
   Always authenticate and authorize based on all available data points, such as user identity, device health, location, and data classification.
2. **Use Least Privilege Access**
   Grant users and systems the minimum access necessary to perform their tasks, limiting potential damage from breaches or errors.
3. **Assume Breach**
   Operate with the assumption that a breach has either already occurred or will occur. Segment networks, monitor systems continuously, and apply real-time analytics to detect abnormal behavior.

Core Components:

- Strong identity and access management (IAM)
- Multi-factor authentication (MFA)
- Device compliance and security posture checks
- Micro-segmentation of networks
- Continuous monitoring and logging

Benefits:

- Reduces the attack surface
- Limits lateral movement of attackers
- Enhances visibility and control over users and devices
- Improves compliance with security regulations

The Zero Trust model (Figure 11) enforces least-privilege access, reducing insider risks.

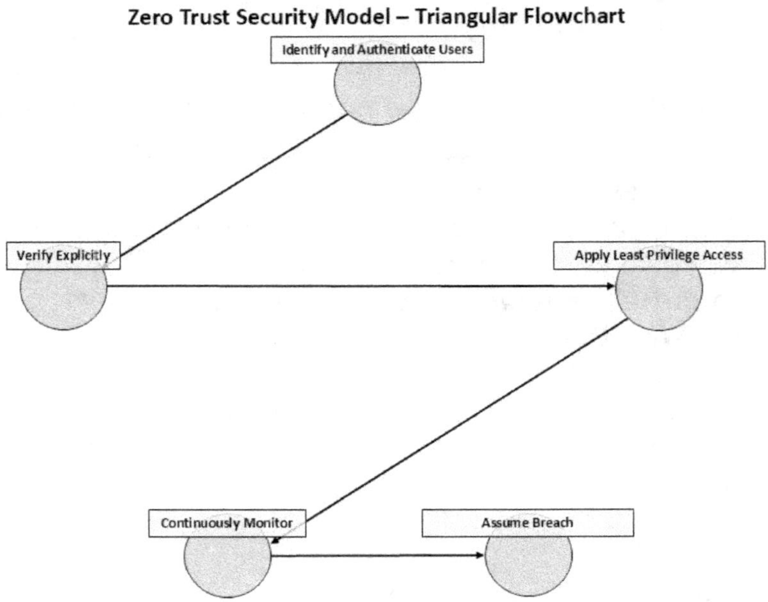

Figure 11. Zero Trust security architecture.

7.5 Regular Security Audits and Penetration Testing

Overview

Conducting regular security audits and penetration testing is vital for uncovering vulnerabilities and mitigating risks before malicious actors can exploit them. These evaluations provide a detailed analysis of the organization's security defenses, offering valuable insights into weaknesses and areas that require improvement. By proactively addressing findings from these assessments, organizations can maintain a strong and resilient security posture.

Key Components

- **Security Audits**: Conducting thorough reviews of security policies, procedures, and controls to ensure they are effective and up-to-date.
- **Penetration Testing**: Simulating real-world attacks to identify vulnerabilities and test the effectiveness of security measures.
- **Vulnerability Scanning**: Using automated tools to scan systems for known vulnerabilities and misconfigurations.

Implementation Tips

- Conduct security audits and penetration testing at least annually, or more frequently for high-risk environments.
- Use the results of audits and tests to prioritize and address vulnerabilities.
- Engage third-party experts to provide an objective assessment of the organization's security posture.

Real-World Example

A healthcare organization conducted regular security audits and penetration testing, which helped identify and address vulnerabilities in its patient data systems. As a result, the organization was able to prevent a potential data breach and ensure compliance with regulatory requirements.

7.6 Incident Response and Recovery Planning

Overview

Having a well-defined incident response and recovery

plan is critical for minimizing the impact of a security breach. The plan outlines the steps to be taken in the event of a breach, including communication protocols, containment measures, and recovery procedures to restore systems and data. This proactive approach empowers organizations to handle crises efficiently while reinforcing their resilience against future threats.

Key Components

- **Incident Detection**: Implementing monitoring and detection systems to identify potential security incidents.
- **Containment and Eradication**: Taking immediate action to contain the incident and eliminate the threat.
- **Communication**: Establishing clear communication protocols for notifying stakeholders, including employees, customers, and regulators.
- **Recovery**: Restoring systems and data to normal operations and conducting a post-incident review to identify lessons learned.

Implementation Tips

- Develop and regularly update the incident response and recovery plan.
- Conduct regular drills and simulations to test the plan and ensure readiness.
- Provide training for incident response team members and other key stakeholders.

Real-World Example

A financial services company experienced a ransomware attack but was able to quickly contain and recover from the incident thanks to its well-prepared incident response plan. The company had clear communication protocols, a trained incident response team, and regular backups, which minimized the impact of the attack.

Conclusion

Mitigating human-related risks in cybersecurity requires a multifaceted approach that combines education, technology, and organizational culture. By implementing strategies such as security awareness training, implementing strong authentication mechanisms, fostering a security-first culture, conducting regular security audits, and developing robust incident response plans collectively empower organizations to lessen human errors and bolster their overall security framework. Addressing the human factor is essential for creating a resilient and secure digital environment.

CHAPTER 8: Policy and Regulatory Considerations

Policy and regulatory frameworks are critical in shaping the cybersecurity landscape. Governments and regulatory bodies establish rules and standards to protect sensitive data, ensure privacy, and promote best practices in cybersecurity. This chapter examines the role of government and regulation, the significance of international cooperation and standards, privacy concerns and ethical considerations, and the impact of key regulations, including the General Data Protection Regulation (GDPR). Understanding these considerations is essential for organizations to ensure compliance, mitigate risks, and build trust with stakeholders.

8.1 The Role of Government and Regulation

Overview

Governments play a pivotal role in cybersecurity by enacting laws and regulations that set minimum standards for data protection, incident reporting, and risk management. These regulations aim to protect individuals, organizations, and national security from cyber threats.

Key Areas of Government Involvement

- **Data Protection Laws**: Regulations such as the GDPR and the California Consumer Privacy Act (CCPA) establish requirements for how organizations collect, store, and process personal data.
- **Incident Reporting**: Many regulations require organizations to report data breaches within a specific timeframe. For example, the GDPR requires breaches to be reported within 72 hours.
- **Critical Infrastructure Protection**: Governments often establish frameworks to protect critical infrastructure, such as energy, healthcare, and financial systems, from cyber threats.

Challenges

- **Compliance Costs**: Meeting regulatory requirements can be costly, particularly for small and medium-sized enterprises (SMEs).
- **Complexity**: Navigating the patchwork of international, national, and industry-specific regulations can be challenging for multinational organizations.
- **Enforcement**: Ensuring compliance and enforcing penalties for non-compliance can be difficult, especially in jurisdictions with limited resources.

Figure 12 aligns regulatory frameworks (e.g., GDPR) with human-centric defenses.

Real-World Example

The GDPR, implemented in 2018, has had a significant impact on global organizations. Companies that fail to comply with GDPR requirements face fines of up to 4% of their annual global turnover or €20 million, whichever is higher. This has prompted organizations to invest heavily in data protection and cybersecurity measures.

Figure 12 aligns regulatory frameworks (e.g., GDPR) with human-centric defenses.

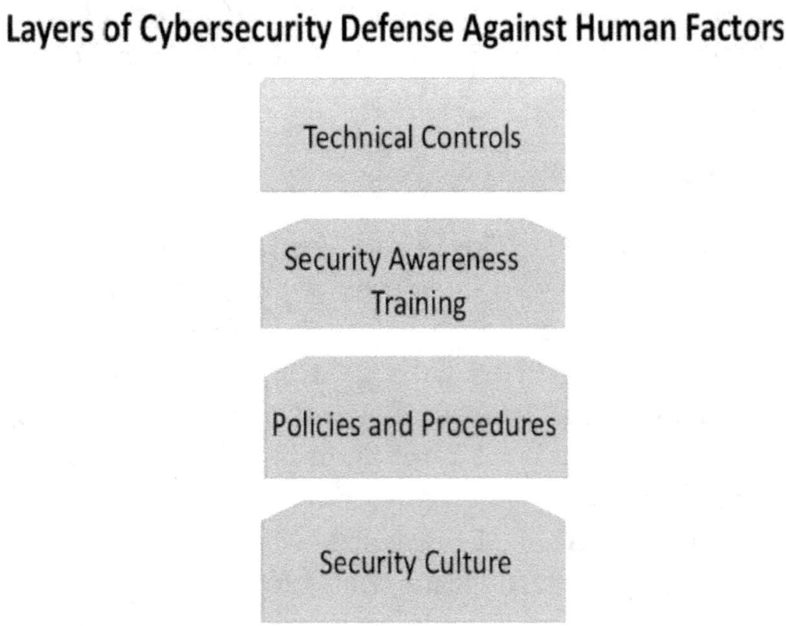

Figure 12. Layered defense model integrating policy and human factors

8.2 International Cooperation and Standards

Overview

Cybersecurity is a global challenge that requires international cooperation and the establishment of unified standards. Organizations like the International Organization for Standardization (ISO) and the National Institute of Standards and Technology (NIST) offers frameworks and guidelines to help organizations effectively identify, assess, and manage cybersecurity risks.

Key International Frameworks

- **ISO/IEC 27001**: A widely recognized standard for information security management systems (ISMS), providing a systematic approach to managing sensitive information.
- **NIST Cybersecurity Framework**: A voluntary framework developed by NIST to help organizations manage and reduce cybersecurity risks.
- **The Budapest Convention**: The first international treaty aimed at addressing cybercrime by harmonizing national laws and improving international cooperation.

Benefits of International Cooperation

- **Consistency**: Common standards and frameworks provide a consistent approach to cybersecurity, making it easier for organizations to comply with multiple regulations.

- **Information Sharing**: International cooperation facilitates sharing threat intelligence and best practices, enhancing global cybersecurity resilience.
- **Capacity Building**: Developing countries can benefit from the expertise and resources of more advanced nations, improving their cybersecurity capabilities.

Real-World Example

The NIST Cybersecurity Framework has been adopted by numerous organizations worldwide, including critical infrastructure sectors in the U.S. The framework provides a flexible and scalable approach to managing cybersecurity risks, making it applicable to organizations of all sizes and industries.

8.3 Privacy Concerns and Ethical Considerations

Overview

The growing reliance on technology in cybersecurity introduces significant privacy and ethical challenges. Organizations must carefully balance their security needs with the obligation to protect individual privacy rights. Additionally, they must uphold ethical standards in their practices, ensuring that security measures are implemented responsibly and transparently to maintain trust and accountability.

Key Privacy and Ethical Issues

- **Data Collection and Surveillance**: The use of surveillance technologies and data collection practices can infringe on individual privacy rights.
- **Bias in AI and Machine Learning**: AI-powered cybersecurity tools can introduce biases, leading to unfair or discriminatory outcomes.
- **Transparency and Accountability**: Organizations must be transparent about their cybersecurity practices and accountable for any breaches or misuse of data.

Mitigation Strategies

- **Privacy by Design**: Incorporate privacy considerations into the design and development of cybersecurity systems and processes.
- **Ethical AI**: Ensure that AI and machine learning algorithms are free from bias and used in an ethical manner.
- **Stakeholder Engagement**: Engage with stakeholders, including employees, customers, and regulators, to address privacy and ethical concerns.

Real-World Example

In 2020, Clearview AI faced significant backlash for its facial recognition technology, which was used by law enforcement agencies without the consent of individuals. The controversy highlighted the importance of ethical considerations in the development and use of cybersecurity technologies.

8.4 The Impact of GDPR and Other Data Protection Laws

Overview

The GDPR, implemented in 2018, has had a profound impact on global cybersecurity practices. It establishes stringent requirements for data protection and imposes significant penalties for non-compliance.

Key Provisions of GDPR

- **Data Subject Rights**: Individuals have the right to access, correct, and delete their personal data, as well as the right to object to its processing.
- **Data Breach Notification**: Organizations must report data breaches to the relevant supervisory authority within 72 hours and notify affected individuals if the breach poses a high risk to their rights and freedoms.
- **Data Protection Officers (DPOs)**: Organizations that process large amounts of personal data must appoint a DPO to oversee compliance with GDPR requirements.

Impact on Organizations

- **Increased Accountability**: Organizations must demonstrate compliance with GDPR requirements through documentation, audits, and risk assessments.

- **Enhanced Data Protection Measures**: The GDPR has prompted organizations to implement stronger data protection measures, such as encryption, access controls, and data minimization.
- **Global Reach**: The GDPR applies to any organization that processes the personal data of EU residents, regardless of where the organization is located.

Real-World Example

In 2019, British Airways was fined £183 million by the UK Information Commissioner's Office (ICO) for a data breach that exposed the personal information of 500,000 customers. The fine was issued under the GDPR, highlighting the regulation's stringent enforcement mechanisms.

Conclusion

Policy and regulatory considerations are vital to building a comprehensive cybersecurity strategy. Governments and regulatory bodies play a crucial role in establishing standards and frameworks that safeguard sensitive data, protect privacy, and promote the adoption of best practices. International collaboration and the establishment of common standards further enhance global cybersecurity resilience. Organizations must navigate complex regulatory requirements, tackle privacy and ethical challenges, and comply with key regulations like the GDPR to thrive in this landscape. By proactively addressing these elements, organizations can create a secure and compliant digital environment.

CHAPTER 9:

Future Trends and Challenges

The cybersecurity landscape is constantly evolving, shaped by rapid technological advancements, emerging threats, and shifting regulatory frameworks. To safeguard their digital assets and maintain a resilient security posture, organizations must remain proactive and adaptable. This chapter delves into future trends and challenges in cybersecurity, including the changing threat landscape, the transformative potential of quantum computing, the implications of IoT and smart devices, and the evolution of cybersecurity education. By gaining insight into these developments, organizations can anticipate challenges, craft effective strategies, and mitigate future risks.

9.1 The Evolving Threat Landscape

Overview

The cybersecurity threat landscape is growing increasingly intricate, as cybercriminals adopt advanced tactics and broaden their scope of targets. Emerging threats include ransomware, supply chain attacks, and nation-state espionage. These developments underscore the need for organizations to continuously adapt their defenses and remain vigilant against evolving risks.

Key Trends

- **Ransomware**: Ransomware attacks are becoming more targeted and damaging, with attackers demanding higher ransoms and exfiltrating data before encrypting it.
- **Supply Chain Attacks**: Cybercriminals are targeting third-party vendors and suppliers to gain access to larger organizations. The SolarWinds attack in 2020 is a prime example of this trend.
- **Nation-State Espionage**: Nation-states are increasingly using cyberattacks for espionage, sabotage, and political influence. These attacks are often highly sophisticated and difficult to detect.

Challenges

- **Detection and Response**: The increasing sophistication of attacks makes it more difficult to detect and respond to threats in a timely manner.
- **Resource Constraints**: Many organizations lack the resources and expertise to defend against advanced threats, particularly SMEs.
- **Regulatory Compliance**: The evolving threat landscape requires organizations to continuously update their security practices to comply with new regulations and standards.

Mitigation Strategies

- Invest in advanced threat detection and response capabilities, such as AI-powered security tools to identify and neutralize attacks in real time.
- Conduct regular risk assessments and penetration testing to identify and address vulnerabilities.
- Collaborate with industry peers and government agencies to share threat intelligence and best practices.

9.2 The Role of Quantum Computing

Overview

Quantum computing holds the transformative potential to reshape the cybersecurity landscape, presenting both challenges and opportunities. On one hand, quantum computers could render traditional encryption algorithms obsolete, exposing sensitive data to vulnerabilities. On the other hand, they pave the way for innovative security solutions, such as quantum-resistant encryption and enhanced cryptographic methods, offering organizations powerful tools to defend against future threats.

Key Trends

- **Quantum Threats**: Quantum computers can solve complex mathematical problems much faster than classical computers, potentially breaking widely used encryption algorithms such as RSA and ECC.

- **Quantum-Resistant Encryption**: Researchers are developing quantum-resistant encryption algorithms to protect against future quantum threats.
- **Quantum Key Distribution (QKD)**: QKD uses the principles of quantum mechanics to create secure communication channels that are theoretically immune to eavesdropping.

Challenges

- **Technological Maturity**: Quantum computing is still in its early stages, and practical quantum computers are not yet widely available.
- **Implementation Costs**: Developing and implementing quantum-resistant encryption and QKD can be costly and complex.
- **Regulatory and Standardization Issues**: The lack of standardized quantum-resistant algorithms and protocols poses challenges for widespread adoption.

Mitigation Strategies

- Stay informed about developments in quantum computing and their potential impact on cybersecurity.
- Initiate preparations for the transition to quantum-resistant encryption, including evaluating and testing new algorithms.
- Collaborate with industry and academic partners to advance research and development in quantum cybersecurity.

9.3 The Impact of IoT and Smart Devices

Overview

The proliferation of IoT and smart devices is revolutionizing the cybersecurity landscape, providing significant conveniences and efficiencies across industries and everyday life. However, this rapid expansion also brings new vulnerabilities and attack vectors. Addressing these risks is critical to ensuring the secure integration of IoT into the digital ecosystem.

Key Trends

- **Increased Attack Surface**: The growing number of connected devices expands the attack surface, providing more opportunities for cybercriminals to exploit vulnerabilities.
- **Lack of Security Standards**: Many IoT devices lack robust security features and are not designed with security in mind, making them easy targets for attackers.
- **Integration Challenges**: Integrating IoT devices with existing IT infrastructure can create security gaps and complicate risk management.

Challenges

- **Device Management**: Managing and securing a vast array of IoT devices can be challenging, particularly in environments with limited resources.
- **Data Privacy**: IoT devices often collect and transmit sensitive data, raising concerns about

data privacy and compliance with regulations such as the GDPR.
- **Supply Chain Risks**: The global nature of IoT supply chains introduces risks, such as the use of compromised components or firmware.

Mitigation Strategies

- Implement strong security controls for IoT devices, including encryption, authentication, and regular firmware updates.
- Develop and enforce security policies for IoT device procurement, deployment, and management.
- Conduct regular security assessments and penetration testing to identify and address vulnerabilities in IoT ecosystems.

9.4 The Future of Cybersecurity Education

Overview

The escalating complexity and prevalence of cyber threats have spurred a surging demand for skilled cybersecurity professionals. Meeting this demand necessitates a robust emphasis on cybersecurity education and workforce development, ensuring individuals are equipped with the expertise and practical experience required to address emerging risks and safeguard critical systems.

Key Trends

- **Skills Gap**: There is a significant shortage of skilled cybersecurity professionals, with millions of unfilled positions worldwide.
- **Diverse Career Paths**: Cybersecurity offers a wide range of career opportunities, from technical roles such as penetration testers and security analysts to strategic roles such as risk managers and chief information security officers (CISOs).
- **Lifelong Learning**: The rapidly evolving nature of cybersecurity requires professionals to engage in continuous learning and professional development.

Challenges

- **Access to Education**: Many individuals, particularly in underserved communities, lack access to quality cybersecurity education and training.
- **Curriculum Development**: Developing and updating cybersecurity curricula to keep pace with emerging threats and technologies is an ongoing challenge.
- **Industry-Academia Collaboration**: Bridging the gap between academia and industry is essential for ensuring that cybersecurity education aligns with real-world needs.

Mitigation Strategies

- Expand access to cybersecurity education through online courses, bootcamps, and partnerships with educational institutions.

- Develop and promote cybersecurity career pathways, including apprenticeships, internships, and certification programs.
- Foster collaboration between academia, industry, and government to align cybersecurity education with workforce needs and emerging trends.

Conclusion

The future of cybersecurity is defined by an ever-changing landscape of threats, rapid technological innovation, and the escalating demand for skilled professionals. Organizations must stay informed about emerging trends and challenges, such as the impact of quantum computing, the proliferation of IoT devices, and the need for cybersecurity education. By proactively addressing these dynamics, organizations can enhance their security posture, reduce risks, and build a resilient digital environment. Navigating this complex landscape requires a strategic blend of cutting-edge technology, forward-thinking planning, and a deep investment in human expertise."

CHAPTER 10: Conclusion

The human factor in cybersecurity is a critical and often underestimated aspect of securing digital systems. While technological solutions are essential, they are not sufficient on their own. Human behavior, decision-making, and interaction significantly influence the effectiveness of cybersecurity measures, acting as both a strength and a vulnerability. This book examined the multifaceted aspects of the human factor, ranging from psychological and behavioral perspectives to real-world case studies, prevalent human errors, and actionable strategies to reduce risks. In this concluding chapter, we summarize the key findings, present final recommendations, and outline the path forward for addressing the human factor in cybersecurity.

10.1 Summary of Key Findings

The Human Factor is the Weakest Link

Human errors, whether due to negligence, lack of awareness, or malicious intent, frequently represent the most vulnerable point in the security chain. Real-world incidents such as the Target data breach, the Equifax breach, and the Wanna Cry ransomware attack highlight the devastating consequences of human-related vulnerabilities.

Psychological and Behavioral Insights

Understanding the psychological and behavioral aspects of human behavior is crucial for addressing the human factor in cybersecurity. Cognitive biases, stress, organizational culture, and social engineering tactics all contribute to human-related risks. By recognizing these factors, organizations can develop targeted strategies to minimize risks.

Technological and Human Interaction

The interaction between humans and technology is a critical aspect of cybersecurity. User interface design, automation, and human-machine collaboration can enhance or undermine security efforts. Organizations must focus on creating user-friendly interfaces, leveraging automation, and fostering collaboration between humans and machines.

Strategies for Mitigating Human-Related Risks

Mitigating human-related risks requires a multifaceted approach that combines education, technology, and organizational culture. Security awareness training, strong authentication mechanisms, fostering a security-first culture, conducting regular security audits, and incident response planning are essential strategies for reducing human-related vulnerabilities.

Policy and Regulatory Considerations

Policy and regulatory frameworks are integral to defining and influencing the cybersecurity landscape. Regulations like the GDPR and frameworks, such as the NIST Cybersecurity Framework, provide guidelines for protecting sensitive data and managing cybersecurity risks. Organizations must navigate the complex regulatory landscape and address privacy and ethical considerations.

Future Trends and Challenges

The cybersecurity landscape is dynamically progressing, with emerging threats, technological advancements, and changing regulatory environments. Organizations must stay informed about future trends and challenges, such as the impact of quantum computing, the surge of IoT devices, and the need for cybersecurity education.

10.2 Final Recommendations

Invest in Security Awareness Training

Regular security awareness training is one of the most effective ways to ameliorate human-related risks. Training programs should cover a range of topics, including phishing awareness, password management, and social engineering. Simulations and exercises can reinforce learning and maintain employee alertness.

Implement Strong Authentication Mechanisms

Strong authentication mechanisms, such as multi-factor authentication (MFA), can significantly reduce the risk of unauthorized access. Organizations should implement MFA for all critical systems and accounts and educate users about its importance.

Foster a Security-First Culture

Creating a security-first culture is essential for minimizing human-related risks. Leaders must demonstrate a commitment to cybersecurity, encourage open communication, and actively recognizing and rewarding behaviors that align with strong security practices.

Conduct Regular Security Audits and Penetration Testing

Regular security audits and penetration testing are essential for identifying and addressing vulnerabilities. Organizations should conduct these assessments at least annually and use the results to prioritize and address risks.

Develop and Maintain an Incident Response Plan

Having a well-defined incident response and recovery plan is critical for minimizing the impact of a security breach. The plan should outline the steps to be taken in the event of a breach, including communication protocols, containment measures, and recovery procedures.

Stay Informed About Emerging Trends and Challenges

Organizations must stay informed about emerging trends and challenges in cybersecurity, such as the impact of quantum computing, the proliferation of IoT devices, and the need for cybersecurity education. Proactively addressing these trends will help organizations stay ahead of the curve.

10.3 The Path Forward

Holistic Approach to Cybersecurity

Addressing the human factor in cybersecurity requires a holistic approach that integrates technology, policy, and human behavior. Organizations must recognize that cybersecurity is not just a technical issue but fundamentally a human one.

Continuous Learning and Adaptation

The rapidly evolving nature of cybersecurity requires organizations to engage in continuous learning and adaptation. Staying informed about emerging threats, technological advancements, and regulatory changes is essential for maintaining a strong security posture.

Collaboration and Information Sharing

Collaboration and information sharing are critical for enhancing global cybersecurity resilience. Organizations should collaborate with industry peers, government agencies, and academic institutions to share threat intelligence and best practices.

Investment in Human Capital

Investing in human capital is key for addressing the human factor in cybersecurity. Organizations must prioritize cybersecurity education and workforce development to build a skilled and knowledgeable workforce.

Building a Resilient Digital Environment

By understanding and addressing the human factor in cybersecurity, organizations can create a resilient and secure digital environment. This requires a combination of technological innovation, strategic planning, and investment in human capital.

Conclusion

The human factor in cybersecurity presents a layered and intricate challenge, demanding a thorough and forward-thinking strategy. By analyzing the psychological and behavioral aspects of human actions, adopting focused strategies to address risks, and keeping pace with emerging trends and challenges, organizations can bolster their security defenses and reduce the likelihood of human-related vulnerabilities. Building a resilient and secure digital environment requires an integrated approach that combines technology, policy frameworks, and an understanding of human behavior. This comprehensive strategy ensures that organizations are well-equipped to address emerging threats and adapt to the evolving cybersecurity landscape. By addressing the human factor, organizations can build trust with stakeholders, protect their digital assets, and navigate the complexities of the cybersecurity landscape.

References

Cialdini, R.B., 2001. *Influence: Science and Practice.* Boston: Allyn & Bacon.

Conger, K., Frenkel, S. and Isaac, M., 2020. *Twitter Hack Raises Questions About Site's Security.* [online] The New York Times. Available at: https://www.nytimes.com [Accessed 12 March 2023].

Council of Europe, 2001. *Budapest Convention on Cybercrime.* [online] Available at: https://www.coe.int [Accessed 25 January 2023].

European Union, 2016. *General Data Protection Regulation (GDPR).* [online] Available at: https://eur-lex.europa.eu [Accessed 3 February 2023].

European Union Agency for Cybersecurity (ENISA), 2021. *Threat Landscape for Supply Chain Attacks.* [online] Available at: https://www.enisa.europa.eu [Accessed 18 April 2023].

Finkle, J. and Baker, L., 2014. *Sony Pictures Suffers Cyber Attack, Studio Cancels 'The Interview' Release.* [online] Reuters. Available at: https://www.reuters.com [Accessed 9 March 2023].

Goodin, D., 2017. *Equifax Hack Was Entirely Preventable, Says House Report.* [online] Ars Technica. Available at: https://arstechnica.com [Accessed 22 February 2023].

Greenberg, A., 2017. *The WannaCry Ransomware*

Attack: What We Know So Far. [online] Wired. Available at: https://www.wired.com [Accessed 14 May 2023].

Hadnagy, C., 2010. *Social Engineering: The Art of Human Hacking.* Hoboken: Wiley.

Information Commissioner's Office (ICO), 2019. *British Airways Fine.* [online] Available at: https://ico.org.uk [Accessed 7 April 2023].

International Information System Security Certification Consortium (ISC)², 2021. *Cybersecurity Workforce Study.* [online] Available at: https://www.isc2.org [Accessed 30 January 2023].

International Organization for Standardization (ISO), 2013. *ISO/IEC 27001: Information Security Management.* [online] Available at: https://www.iso.org [Accessed 19 March 2023].

Kahneman, D., 2011. *Thinking, Fast and Slow.* New York: Farrar, Straus and Giroux.

Krebs, B., 2014. *Target Hackers Broke in Via HVAC Company.* [online] Krebs on Security. Available at: https://krebsonsecurity.com [Accessed 5 February 2023].

Kruger, J. and Dunning, D., 1999. Unskilled and Unaware of It: How Difficulties in Recognizing One's Own Incompetence Lead to Inflated Self-Assessments. *Journal of Personality and Social Psychology,* 77(6), pp.1121–1134.

McKinsey & Company, 2021. *The Internet of Things: Catching up to an Accelerating Opportunity.* [online] Available at: https://www.mckinsey.com [Accessed 27 April 2023].

Morgan, S., 2020. *Cybercrime To Cost The World $10.5 Trillion Annually By 2025.* [online] Cybersecurity Ventures. Available at: https://cybersecurityventures.com [Ac cessed 10 May 2023].

National Institute of Standards and Technology (NIST), 2018. *NIST Cybersecurity Framework*. [online] Available at: https://www.nist.gov [Accessed 15 January 2023].

National Institute of Standards and Technology (NIST), 2020. *Post-Quantum Cryptography*. [online] Available at: https://www.nist.gov [Accessed 8 March 2023].

Reason, J., 1990. *Human Error*. Cambridge: Cambridge University Press.

Schneier, B., 2000. *Secrets and Lies: Digital Security in a Networked World*. Hoboken: Wiley.

Tversky, A. and Kahneman, D., 1974. Judgment under Uncertainty: Heuristics and Biases. *Science*, 185(4157), pp.1124–1131.

Turton, W., 2021. *Colonial Pipeline Hackers Stole Data Before Shutdown*. [online] Bloomberg. Available at: https://www.bloomberg.com [Accessed 21 April 2023].

Verizon, 2023. *2023 Data Breach Investigations Report*. [online] Available at: https://www.verizon.com/business/resources/reports/dbir/ [Accessed 2 May 2023].

World Economic Forum, 2020. *The Global Risks Report 2020*. [online] Available at: https://www.weforum.org [Accessed 16 February 2023].

www.ingramcontent.com/pod-product-compliance
Lightning Source LLC
LaVergne TN
LVHW022306200926
848481LV00004B/1232
* 9 7 8 9 7 6 9 7 4 1 3 9 3 *